30 DOUGH CRAFT CREATIONS

Inspirational projects with salt dough

ULTIMATE
EDITIONS

First published in 1997 by Ultimate Editions

© 1997 Anness Publishing Limited

Ultimate Editions is an imprint of
Anness Publishing Limited
Hermes House
88-89 Blackfriars Road
London SE1 8HA

ISBN 1 86035 232 4

Distributed in Canada by Book Express, an imprint of
Raincoast Books Distribution Limited

Publisher: Joanna Lorenz
Project Editor: Fiona Eaton
Designer: Lilian Lindblom
Illustrations: Anna Koska

1 3 5 7 9 10 8 6 4 2

Printed in China

CONTENTS

INTRODUCTION

All the lovely sculpted and moulded designs in this collection are made from three of the most basic substances in our lives: flour, salt and water. The technique of modelling dough has been around for centuries, with its obvious connections with bread-making: the ancient Egyptians, Greeks and Romans all used it to make offerings to the gods. It became popular as a decorative craft in nineteenth-century Germany, when salt was added to the dough to prevent the little ornaments being nibbled by mice. It's also a thriving folk-art tradition in South America, producing exuberant designs which are the inspiration for some of the colourful projects in this book.

Salt dough is cheap and easy to make and requires very little in the way of equipment: you probably already have most of the things you will need to make it in the kitchen cupboard.

You'll find the basic recipe for making the dough on page 62. If you prefer, you can use an electric mixer or a food processor to make the job even speedier.

Baking times are given for each project, but these do vary and you need to make sure that your model is completely hard all over before leaving it to cool. You can tint or marble the dough before you shape it, paint it with subtle water-colours or vibrant acrylics after baking, sponge it, gild it or leave it plain, but always protect your creations with several coats of varnish.

Children love making models with salt dough, and it's very safe for them to use as, like the mice, they won't be tempted to eat it. Pastry moulds and cutters are great fun for children to use and make very satisfying models. You'll find plenty of ideas here to enchant craft enthusiasts of all ages.

FLOWER VASE

This vibrant bottomless vase with its star-shaped rim is designed to be placed over a jar of water which can then be filled with flowers. Do not splash water on the vase, as this may damage the dough.

MATERIALS

1 quantity salt dough
rolling pin
section of large cardboard poster tube about 30 cm (12 in) long
baking parchment
baking tray
small, sharp knife
paintbrushes
acrylic gesso or matt emulsion (flat latex) paint
acrylic or craft paints
satin varnish

1 Roll the dough out to a thickness of 1.5 cm (⅝ in) and cover one half of the cardboard tube. Make sure you cover the inside as well as the outside of the tube. Transfer the tube, on baking parchment, to a baking tray and bake at 120°C/250°F/Gas ½ for about 1 hour.

2 Cover the remaining part of the tube with dough, smoothing down the joins with a moistened finger. Return the tube to the oven for another hour. Re-roll the remaining dough to a thickness of about 1 cm (½ in) and cut out eight triangles. Transfer these, on baking parchment, to a baking tray, and bake for 3 hours until hard.

3 When the pieces are cool, smear dough around the rim of the vase and stick on the triangles, using a little water to help them stick. Smooth down any visible joins with a moistened finger. Return the vase to the oven, standing upright, for a further 12 hours.

4 When the vase is cool, paint on an undercoat of acrylic gesso or matt emulsion (flat latex) paint and leave to dry. Decorate the vase with acrylic or craft paints and leave to dry. Apply five coats of satin varnish.

METAL-EMBEDDED BOWLS

These rustic bowls have the appearance of weather-worn stone. The qualities of metal provide an exciting source of decorative materials to use with salt dough – here coins, bronze decorations for making jewellery, wire and motifs cut from copper sheet have been used.

MATERIALS

(to make two bowls)
vegetable oil
2 oven-proof bowls
2 x quantity salt dough
rolling pin
small, sharp knife
metal jewellery accessories,
bonsai wire, coins, etc.
thin copper sheet
scissors
pencil
pair of compasses
paper
baking parchment
baking tray
ruler
paintbrushes
watercolour paints
metallic craft paints
natural sponge
satin varnish
strong, clear glue
jewellery stones

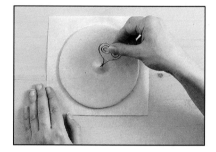

1 Oil the upturned bowls. Divide the dough in half and roll each piece out to a thickness of 1 cm (½ in). Carefully lift each piece of dough and place it over a bowl, smoothing it down. Cut the edges level. Press your chosen metal pieces into the dough. Cut spirals from thin copper sheet using old scissors. Bake at 120°C/250°F/Gas ½ for 9 hours, removing the oven-proof bowls once the dough has hardened sufficiently.

2 To make a lid, cut a paper circle 2 cm (¾ in) wider than the dough bowl. Roll out the remaining dough on baking parchment to a thickness of 1 cm (½ in) and use the template to cut a circle. Fix a ball of dough in the centre. Coil two lengths of bonsai wire to make a heart-shaped handle and insert into the centre of the lid. Transfer the lid, on the parchment, to a baking tray and bake for 5 hours.

3 Measure the inner diameter of the bowl and cut out a paper circle 1 cm (½ in) smaller than this. Use as a template to cut a circle from rolled-out dough. Upturn the baked lid and support it on the oven-proof bowl. Moisten the underside of the lid and fix the smaller circle in place to form the lip of the lid. Return to the oven for 5 hours.

4 Paint the bowls and lid with watercolours, using muted colours and blending them together. Dab the bowls with metallic craft paints, using a natural sponge. Wipe any paint off the metal immediately. Apply five coats of satin varnish, including the metal decorations and base of the handle. Glue jewellery stones to the metal decorations.

FRINGED BOXES

Marbling produces an endless variety of patterns, depending on how many colours are used and how thoroughly the dough is kneaded.

MATERIALS

yellow and blue food colourings
1 quantity salt dough
rolling pin
baking parchment
small, sharp knife
ruler
drinking straw
baking tray
fine-grade sandpaper
books or weights
string
paintbrush
satin varnish
gold cord
4 gold tassels
scissors

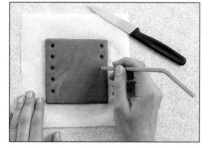

1 Using the food colourings, colour half the dough yellow and half blue. Roll each piece into a sausage and twist together, kneading to blend the colours. Roll out on baking parchment to a thickness of 8 mm (⅛ in). Cut four 10 cm (4 in) squares for the sides and one 9.5 cm (3¾ in) square for the base. Punch rows of five holes down each side piece using a drinking straw. Transfer the squares, on the parchment, to a baking tray and bake at 120°C/250°F/Gas ½ for 5½ hours.

2 Sand the backs and sides of the squares. Moisten the edges of the base and smear with dough. Moisten the lower edges of the side squares and fix against the base. Support with books or weights. Smear dough along the joins inside the box. Tie string around the box to hold the sides in place. Return to the oven for 2 hours. Smear more dough along the joins under the base and bake for a further 3 hours. Remove the string and apply five coats of satin varnish.

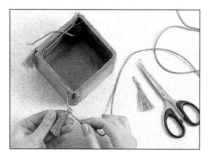

3 Lace the cord through the holes, threading on a tassel at the top of each corner. Cut off the tassels' hanging loops and adjust to hang between the holes. Fasten the ends of the cord together inside the box.

NEEDLEWORK CASKET

*A lidded bowl makes a practical container for all kinds of small objects.
The delicately painted flowers on this needlework casket resemble pretty
embroidery motifs.*

MATERIALS

3 x quantity salt dough
rolling pin
vegetable oil
oven-proof bowl
small, sharp knife
pair of compasses
pencil
thin card (cardboard)
scissors
masking tape
skewer
baking parchment
baking tray
paintbrushes
acrylic gesso or matt emulsion
(flat latex) paint
acrylic or craft paints
satin varnish
small gold bead
thick wire
large ceramic bead

TIP

The proportions of the lid will depend on the size you cut the disc for the mould and how much you overlap the cut edges. As a guide, a 24 cm (9½ in) circle was cut for this 18 cm (7 in) bowl.

1 Roll the dough out to a thickness of 1 cm (½ in). Oil the upturned oven-proof bowl and carefully smooth the dough over the bowl. Cut the edges level. To make a conical mould for the lid, cut out a circle from thin card (cardboard). Cut a slit to the centre. Overlap the straight edges to form a cone that sits comfortably on the bowl. Secure with masking tape and coat with oil. Roll out the remaining dough to a thickness of about 1 cm (½ in) and cover the cone.

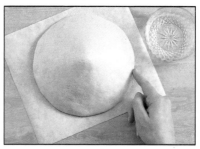

2 Cut away the excess dough and smooth the edge. Pierce a hole in the point of the cone with a skewer. Transfer the lid, on baking parchment, to a baking tray, and bake it and the bowl at 120°C/250°F/Gas ½ for 7 hours. Remove the moulds and bake for a further 2 hours. When baked, allow the dough to cool.

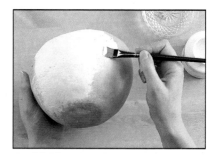

3 Undercoat the bowl and lid with acrylic gesso or matt emulsion (flat latex) paint. Decorate with acrylic or craft paints. Paint the inside of the bowl and lid in a contrasting colour, adding simple motifs at random. Allow to dry.

4 Apply five coats of satin varnish.
Thread a small gold bead on to
a 15 cm (6 in) length of wire, bend
the wire ends downwards like a hair-
pin and thread on a large ceramic
bead. Insert the wire ends into the
hole in the lid and splay them open
inside to hold the beads in place.

CITRUS FRUIT PLATES

Use warm, glowing colours for these plates to enhance the Mediterranean feel of the orange and lemon borders. The very realistic fruits and leaves are easy to model, and a final coating of satin varnish creates the soft sheen of luscious fruit.

MATERIALS

(to make two plates)
vegetable oil
2 oven-proof plates, about 21.5 cm
(8 ½ in) in diameter
2 x quantity salt dough
rolling pin
small, sharp knife
baking parchment
baking tray
paintbrushes
watercolour paints
satin varnish

TIP

The fruity theme of these plates can be varied as you wish. Try experimenting with bunches of grapes, clusters of strawberries or blueberries. Vegetables, too, would provide attractive themes, especially highly coloured peppers, chillies, carrots or tomatoes.

1 Oil the plates. Divide the dough in half, and roll each piece out to a thickness of 5 mm (¼ in). Carefully lift the dough pieces and place one over each plate. Cut away the excess and smooth the cut edges. Reserve the trimmings.

2 Indent crosses at random on the dough using the tip of the knife. Roll out the remaining dough to a thickness of about 5 mm (¼ in). Cut out 12 leaf shapes for each plate and indent the veins.

3 Working on baking parchment, roll nine 2.5 cm (1 in) balls of dough for the oranges and nine for the lemons. Squeeze the ends of the lemons. Transfer the fruit and leaves, on the parchment, to a baking tray and bake at 120°C/250°F/Gas ½ for 1 hour. Moisten the undersides of the leaves and fruit, smear with dough and press on to the rims of the plates. Bake for 9 hours, removing the plate moulds when the top of the dough is completely hard. Paint with watercolour paints, then apply five coats of satin varnish.

MEXICAN BOX

*Painted in rich vibrant colours, this box is designed to hang on the wall,
and makes a handy container for kitchen implements.*

MATERIALS

tracing paper
pencil
card (cardboard) or paper for templates
scissors
5 x quantity salt dough
rolling pin
baking parchment
small, sharp knife
fruit corer
baking tray
non-stick tart tray (muffin pan)
dressmaker's pin
fine-grade sandpaper
books or weights
string
paintbrushes
acrylic gesso or matt emulsion
(flat latex) paint
acrylic or craft paints
satin varnish
coloured raffia
strong, clear glue

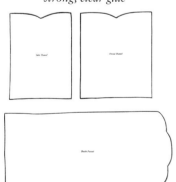

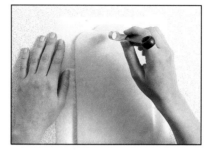

1 Scale up and cut out templates
for the box. Roll the dough out
on baking parchment to a thickness
of 1 cm (½ in). Use the templates to
cut the back, two sides and front.
Cut out a square for the base, to
match the width of a side panel.
Punch a hole in the centre top of the
back using a fruit corer. Transfer the
pieces to a baking tray and bake at
120°C/250°F/Gas ½ for 1 hour.

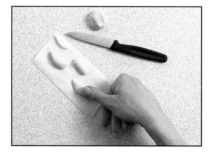

2 To make a sombrero, roll two
balls of dough, each about 3 cm
(1¼ in) in diameter. Flatten one ball
for the brim and to mould it, press
into the cup of a tart tray (muffin
pan). Flatten the base of the second
ball and gently squeeze the top into a
blunt point. Fix to the brim. Make
two more sombreros, place them on
baking parchment and bake for
2¼ hours.

3 Mould four balls of dough, 1-1.5 cm
(½-⅝ in) in diameter, into flat oval
shapes and press together to form a
cactus. Press on three tiny balls for the
flowers and indent with a pin head.
Prick the cactus to suggest spines.
Make six more cacti. Make nine chilli
peppers from 2 cm (¾ in) diameter
balls. Roll sausages for stalks. Moisten
one end and press against the
chillies, curving one in the opposite
direction. Bake the cacti and chillies
for 25 minutes until slightly hardened.

4 Moisten the surfaces and attach the motifs to the box with raw dough. Return to the oven, with the box base, for 18 hours. Sand the edges. Moisten the edges of the base and smear them with dough. Moisten the inner edges of the back, sides and front and assemble the box. Support the panels with books or weights as you position them. Tie string around the box to hold all the panels in place and return to the oven for 3 hours. Sand along the joins. Undercoat the box with acrylic gesso or matt emulsion (flat latex) paint, then paint with acrylic or craft paints. Apply five coats of satin varnish. Tie a piece of raffia around each sombrero and secure with strong, clear glue.

STRING & SHELL BOWLS

*You can use salt dough to make a range of bowls, using different moulds,
textures and applied decorations.*

MATERIALS

(to make two bowls)
vegetable oil
2 oven-proof bowls
2 x quantity salt dough
rolling pin
small, sharp knife
shells
string
baking parchment
baking tray
paintbrushes
acrylic gesso or matt emulsion
(flat latex) paint
acrylic or craft paints
matt varnish

TIP

Paint the bowls in bright exuberant
colours or, for a more natural
style, leave them unpainted and
simply apply a few coats of varnish
for protection.

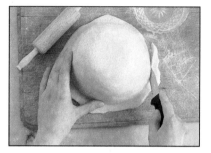

1 Oil the upturned bowls. Divide
the dough in half, and roll each
half out to a thickness of 1 cm
(½ in). Carefully lift the dough and
mould it on to the outside of both
the bowls. Cut away the excess
dough and smooth the edge.

3 To decorate the string bowl,
wind the string around the bowl,
pushing it gently into the dough.
Transfer the bowls, on baking parchment, to a baking tray, and bake at
120°C/250°F/Gas ½ for 12 hours.
Remove the bowl moulds when cool.

2 To decorate the shell bowl, press
a selection of clean shells gently
into the dough. Smooth the dough
around the shells with a moistened
finger to help keep them in place.
Do not press too hard or you may
push the shells through the dough.

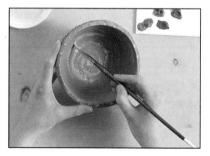

4 Paint on an undercoat of acrylic
gesso or matt emulsion (flat
latex) paint, then decorate with
acrylic or craft paints. Apply five
coats of matt varnish.

CROWN LETTER RACK

*For a different finished look, you could emphasize the regal theme by painting
the base deep red or purple and the crowns in glittering gold.*

MATERIALS

*1 quantity salt dough
rolling pin
baking parchment
pencil
card (cardboard) or paper for templates
scissors
small, sharp knife
paintbrushes
baking tray
fine-grade sandpaper
acrylic gesso or matt emulsion
(flat latex) paint
acrylic or craft paints
satin varnish*

1 Roll the dough out on baking parchment to a thickness of 1 cm (½ in). Draw a crown and a base shape to the size required and cut out of card (cardboard) or paper. Using these templates as a guide, cut the dough, making three crown shapes.

2 Roll nine 1.5 cm (⅝ in) diameter balls and flatten them. Moisten the crowns and press the balls in place. Indent them with a paintbrush. Transfer, on baking parchment, to a baking tray and bake at 120°C/250°F/Gas ½ for 5 hours.

3 Smooth edges with sandpaper. Attach each crown to its base using tacky salt dough. Smooth joins. Return to the oven for 2 hours. When cool, paint with gesso or matt emulsion (flat latex) paint, then decorate. Apply five coats of satin varnish.

Spiky Napkin Ring

Paint these eye-catching napkin rings to co-ordinate with your china and table linen; you could also personalize them with names or initials.

MATERIALS
....

scissors
cardboard tube
½ quantity salt dough
rolling pin
baking parchment
baking tray
fine-grade sandpaper
paintbrushes
acrylic gesso or matt emulsion
(flat latex) paint
acrylic or craft paints
matt varnish

1 Cut a 6 cm (2¼ in) length of cardboard tube. Roll the dough out to a thickness of about 5 mm (¼ in). Slightly dampen the tube and cover it inside and out with dough, smoothing down all the joins with a moistened finger.

2 Mould the spikes from nine 2.5 cm (1 in) diameter balls of dough. Transfer the spikes and the ring, on baking parchment, to a baking tray and bake at 120°C/ 250°F/Gas ½ for 45 minutes.

3 Stick the spikes on to the ring with raw dough. Smooth the joins with a moistened finger and bake for a further 9 hours. Lightly sand the napkin ring and paint on a coat of acrylic gesso or matt emulsion (flat latex) paint, then decorate. Apply five coats of matt varnish.

BRAIDED CANDLEHOLDER

This candleholder has a charming rustic feel and is made with interwoven braids of dough forming a circular base. If you like the natural colour, you can finish it off simply with a few coats of matt varnish.

MATERIALS

*shallow 15 cm (6 in) diameter
oven-proof dish with wide rim
baking parchment
vegetable oil
1 quantity salt dough
rolling pin
6 cm (2¼ in) round pastry
(cookie) cutter
small, sharp knife
paintbrush
matt varnish*

1 Line the dish with baking parchment and coat with a thin layer of oil. Roll out the dough to a thickness of about 5 mm (¼ in), and cut a circle with a pastry (cookie) cutter to make a base for the candlestick. Roll the remaining dough into sausage shapes about 8 mm (⅜ in) thick.

2 Cut sausage shapes into lengths of about 15 cm (6 in). Arrange 16 of these around the centre circle of dough at regular intervals, leaving sufficient space in the centre for a candle. Press the dough gently in place. Then add another 16 lengths between those in the first layer.

3 Working in pairs, weave the lengths of dough by placing each alternate roll over the one next to it. Continue to interlace the rolls, placing every other one over the adjacent roll. Work all around the dish and repeat twice.

4 Trim the end of each roll and tuck under to form a neat rim. Make the candleholder from two short rolls of dough formed into rings and placed centrally, one on top of the other. Bake the candlestick at 120°C/250°F/Gas ½ for 6 hours, until it is hard. Finish by applying five coats of matt varnish.

MEXICAN TREE OF LIFE

This wonderful model looks very complex, but is in fact quite straightforward to make. The tree itself is left unpainted, to contrast with the assortment of bright flowers and exotic creatures on its branches.

MATERIALS

wire coat hanger
wire cutters
narrow masking tape
baking parchment
1 quantity salt dough
small, sharp knife
knitting needle
medium-weight wire
modelling tool
glass-headed dressmaker's pins
aluminium foil
baking tray
paintbrushes
watercolour inks
satin and matt varnish

1 The tree is built up over a wire armature (frame) which supports its branches during and after baking. Make this from lengths cut from a coat hanger, bound together with narrow masking tape.

2 Working on baking parchment, cover the wire armature (frame) completely with a layer of dough, shaping the ends of the branches into points. Smooth over the joins with a moistened finger.

3 Form the serpent from a tapered roll of dough. Cut a small slit at the head end and insert a pea-sized ball of dough for an apple. Mark the eye with a knitting needle, moisten the dough and coil the snake around the trunk.

4 Shape individual leaves on short lengths of medium-weight wire. Indent the leaf surfaces slightly with a modelling tool and mark the veins with a knife tip. Insert the wires into the dough branches, securing each with a small collar of dough.

5 Build up the flowers, petal by petal. Roll small balls of dough, pinch them into diamond shapes and press together. Decorate the centres with small balls of dough and indent the petals with the knitting needle.

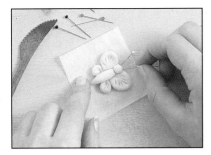

6 Make the bee and butterfly by rolling small round heads and sausage-shaped bodies. To make the wings, roll small balls of dough and flatten them. Moisten and press on to the bodies. Use glass-headed dressmaker's pins as antennae.

7 Attach the flowers and insects to the trunk with wire stalks. Make a dove if you wish, using the picture as a guide. For support, place pads of foil under the flowers. Transfer, on the parchment, to a baking tray and bake at 120°C/250°F/Gas ½ for 10 hours. Paint with watercolour inks, leaving the trunk unpainted. Coat the painted areas with five coats of satin varnish and the trunk with five coats of matt varnish.

FLYING ANGEL

This angel has charming curly hair, a cheeky smile and a heart emblazoned on its chest. Once you have mastered the basic template, you can create all sorts of delightful cherub variations.

MATERIALS

tracing paper
pencil
baking parchment
1 quantity salt dough
modelling tool
ruler
rolling pin
dressmaker's pin
small heart-shaped cutter
paperclip
wire cutters
baking tray
paintbrushes
acrylic gesso or matt emulsion
(flat latex) paint
acrylic or craft paints
matt varnish

TIP
Make tiny gilded cherubs using this technique, thread them with lengths of gold cord and hang them on your Christmas tree.

1 Scale up the template and transfer to a 20 cm (8 in) square of baking parchment. First make the wings by rolling curved sausages of dough and laying them between the traced outlines. Roll a 3 cm (1¼ in) ball of dough to form the head and flatten it slightly. Moisten the inner edge of the right wing and place the head in position.

2 Mould the body shape, moisten the top edges and join to the head and wings. Smooth the edges with a modelling tool. The angel's hair is formed from small coils of dough, of various sizes, arranged around the head. Mark the eyes and mouth with a dressmaker's pin.

3 Cut out a small heart. Moisten the underside and press it into place. Make the feet from pea-sized balls of dough, pressed into triangles. Snip the paperclip in half with wire cutters and press it into the top of the head. Transfer the angel, on the baking parchment, to a baking tray, and bake at 120°C/250°F/Gas ½ for 10 hours. Allow to cool. Undercoat with acrylic gesso or matt emulsion (flat latex) paint, then decorate. Apply five coats of matt varnish.

TEAPOT CLOCK

*Just the thing to cheer up early morning breakfasts, this delightful clock face is
decorated to resemble a traditional blue and white china teapot.*

MATERIALS

*small oven-proof plate
aluminium foil
vegetable oil
baking parchment
2 x quantity salt dough
rolling pin
small, sharp knife
small trefoil (shamrock) cutter
skewer
baking tray
florist's wire
paintbrushes
acrylic gesso or matt emulsion
(flat latex) paint
cream and blue acrylic paints
satin varnish
clock movement and hands*

1 Cover the underside of the plate with foil. Pad out the centre if necessary to raise it slightly. Oil the foil and place on baking parchment. Roll out a circle of dough to a thickness of 1 cm (½ in) and lay over the foil. Trim to fit and cut a circle in the centre for the spindle.

2 Roll sausage shapes for the lid rim and base, and a ball for the knob. Dampen both surfaces before positioning the pieces and press them into place.

5 Return to the oven for 4 hours. Allow to cool and remove the plate. Undercoat the clock with acrylic gesso or matt emulsion (flat latex) paint. When dry, paint with cream acrylic. Paint the flowers pale blue and pick out the details in dark blue. Apply five coats of varnish. Fit the clock movement and hands.

3 Shape and add the spout. Mark with a trefoil (shamrock) cutter and a skewer; position the flowers to represent the clock numerals. Prick a dot pattern along the lid and base.

4 Transfer to a baking tray and bake at 120°C/250°F/Gas ½ for 1 hour. Cool. Bend a length of florist's wire into a handle and cover with dough. Moisten and fix in place.

WINGED HEART

This wall decoration is a charming way to tell someone that you are thinking
of them – with a heart that has, literally, taken wing.

MATERIALS

tracing paper
pencil
card (cardboard) or paper for template
scissors
1 quantity salt dough
baking parchment
rolling pin
small, sharp knife
modelling tool
small heart-shaped cutter
aluminium foil
small natural sponge
baking tray
2 screw eyes
paintbrushes
acrylic gesso or matt emulsion
(flat latex) paint
acrylic or craft paints
gloss varnish
picture cord

1 Scale up the template, trace the
outlines of the design on to it and
cut out. Roll out about two-thirds of
the dough on a sheet of baking parchment to a thickness of 8 mm (⅜ in).
Put the template on the dough and
cut around it with a knife. Make thin
rolls of dough, moisten the edges and
press them around the border. Smooth
the joins with a modelling tool and
cut out a small heart for each corner.

2 Using the template, shape the
foil into a heart. Roll out half
the remaining dough to a thickness
of 5 mm (¼ in) and place it over the
foil heart. Trim the edges and centre
the background. Smooth with a
damp sponge. Roll out the remaining
dough and cut out the wings. Mark
the feathers with a modelling tool.
Moisten the backs and put them on
the background. Smooth the edges.

3 Transfer the panel, on the
baking parchment, to a baking
tray and bake at 120°C/250°F/Gas ½
for 2 hours. Fix the screw eyes on
the back. Bake for at least 6 hours.
Allow to cool. Undercoat with
acrylic gesso or matt emulsion (flat
latex) paint. Paint the hearts red, the
wings white and the background
black, then decorate. Finish with five
coats of varnish. When dry, thread
the cord through the screw eyes.

SPONGED GOOSE KEYRACK

This colourful keyrack makes a pretty, rustic wall decoration as well as being
a practical place to keep those household keys that always seem to go astray.

tracing paper
pencil
2 x quantity salt dough
rolling pin
baking parchment
small, sharp knife
dressmaker's pin
modelling tool
toy glass eye or black bead
4 small brass hooks
baking tray
2 eyelet loops
paintbrushes
acrylic gesso or matt emulsion
(flat latex) paint
small natural sponge
acrylic or craft paints
matt varnish
picture wire

1 Scale up the template and transfer to tracing paper. Roll the dough out on baking parchment to a thickness of 1 cm (½ in). Cut around the template, and transfer the details by pricking with a pin. Using a moistened finger, smooth the cut edges. Then use a modelling tool or the tip of a knife to define the lines on the goose wings and body. Press the glass eye or bead into place on the head.

2 Roll a 15 x 1 cm (6 x ½ in) sausage from the remaining dough, moisten it and attach to the lower edge of the model. Use a modelling tool or knife to mark the reeds. Push four hooks into this supporting roll. Transfer the model, on the parchment, to a baking tray and bake at 120°C/250°F/Gas ½ for 2 hours. Remove from the oven and insert two eyelet loops into the back. Bake for a further 10 hours.

3 When cool, paint the whole model with a base coat of acrylic gesso or matt emulsion (flat latex) paint. When dry, apply stippled and sponged colour using a dry brush and a small natural sponge. Leave to dry, then apply five coats of matt varnish. Fix a length of wire between the eyelets on the back for hanging.

Mosaic Mirror

This exciting mirror design creates multiple views of your reflection,
with the blue of the frame setting off each embedded shard of glass. The
original brightness of the blue colouring will gently fade over time.

MATERIALS

pencil
card (cardboard) or paper for templates
scissors
blue food colouring
4 x quantity salt dough
rolling pin
baking parchment
three 15 cm (6 in) mirror tiles
small, sharp knife
old towel
hammer
baking tray
aluminium foil
masking tape
fine-grade sandpaper
paintbrush
satin varnish

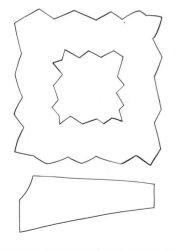

1 Scale up the templates and cut out, including the centre of the frame. Knead the food colouring into the dough. Divide the dough in half and roll each half out on a piece of baking parchment to a thickness of 1 cm (½ in). Press a mirror tile centrally on to one piece of the rolled dough.

2 Use the template to cut out the mirror frame on the second piece of rolled dough. Lift the frame, on the parchment, and place it face down on the first piece, positioning the cut-out over the mirror. Peel off the parchment. Cut away the lower section of dough around the outer edges of the frame. Smooth the edges and surface with a moistened finger.

3 Wrap the remaining mirror tiles in a towel and smash with a hammer (discard the towel). Arrange the fragments on the frame, then press into the dough. Smooth the dough over the edges with a finger. Roll out the remaining dough on baking parchment to a thickness of 1 cm (½ in) and cut out the stand. Bake the frame at 120°C/250°F/ Gas ½ for 24 hours and the stand for 12 hours. Allow to cool.

4 To attach the stand, moisten the shorter of the long edges and smear with dough. With the mirror face down, dampen the back along the centre and press the stand on top. Spread more dough along the join. Support with scrunched up aluminium foil held in place with masking tape, and return to the oven for 3 hours. Allow to cool, then sand carefully along the join. Apply five coats of satin varnish to the frame, avoiding the mirror.

TREE PLAQUES

Create a menagerie of cheerful creatures to decorate your home during the festive season. Salt-dough tree decorations were very popular in nineteenth-century Germany, and they are just as appealing today.

MATERIALS

tracing paper
pencil
card (cardboard) or paper for templates
scissors
1 quantity salt dough
rolling pin
baking parchment
small, sharp knife
ruler
fruit corer
drinking straw
baking tray
fine-grade sandpaper
paintbrushes
watercolour paints
metallic craft paints
satin varnish
ribbon

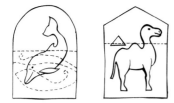

1 Scale up the templates to the size required and cut out of card (cardboard) or paper. Roll the dough out on baking parchment to a thickness of 5 mm (¼ in). Place the templates on the dough and cut around them. Carefully indent the broken lines of the template through to the dough with the tip of a knife.

2 From the remaining rolled-out dough, cut strips 5 mm (¼ in) wide for the frames, using a ruler to keep the edges even. Moisten the edges of the plaques and position the strips, mitring the corners. Place the pyramid and animal templates on the remaining dough and cut out the shapes. Cut the head off the cheetah. Round all the cut edges.

3 Mould a diamond for the camel's ear. Moisten and press on to the head. Moisten the cheetah's head and press it on to the body, overlapping the neck. Cut out a fin for the dolphin and a tiny triangle for the cheetah's nose. Indent facial features and other details. Cut four circles of dough with a fruit corer; use one for the sun on the cheetah plaque. Punch holes in the other three with a drinking straw and fix one to the top of each plaque.

4 Transfer the pieces, on the parchment, to a baking tray and bake at 120°C/250°F/Gas ½ for 1 hour. Allow to cool. Moisten the undersides of the cut-out shapes and smear with dough. Moisten the plaques and press the pieces gently in position. Return them to the oven for a further 9 hours. Allow to cool, then lightly sand the edges.

5 Paint the models with water-colour paints. Paint the stars on the camel plaque with metallic paint, using a fine paintbrush. Apply five coats of satin varnish. Thread ribbon through the rings to hang up the plaques.

SPECTACULAR STAR FRAME

Transform a plain picture frame by decorating it with brightly painted cut-out stars. Different colours and patterns have been used on each star, but all follow the same dotty theme.

MATERIALS

pencil
card (cardboard) or paper for template
scissors
1 quantity salt dough
rolling pin
baking parchment
small, sharp knife
baking tray
fine-grade sandpaper
paintbrushes
acrylic gesso or matt emulsion
(flat latex) paint
acrylic or craft paints
MDF (medium-density fiberboard)
frame
strong, clear glue
satin varnish

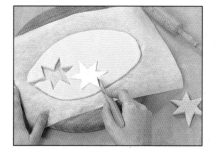

1 Draw a freehand star shape on card (cardboard) or paper and cut out to use as a template. Roll out the dough on baking parchment to a thickness of 8 mm (⅜ in). Cut out eight stars. Transfer, on the parchment, to a baking tray and bake at 120°C/250°F/Gas ½ for 5 hours.

2 Allow the stars to cool, then sand them with fine-grade sandpaper until ready for painting.

3 Paint each star with acrylic gesso or matt emulsion (flat latex) paint and allow to dry. Decorate the stars with acrylic or craft paints.

4 Fix the stars on to the frame using strong, clear glue. Finish with five coats of satin varnish.

FOLK ANGEL

A heralding angel is a familiar symbol of American folk art. This charming
example, perhaps hung from a fine ribbon, would make a delightful
house-warming gift.

MATERIALS

1 quantity salt dough
rolling pin
baking parchment
pencil
tracing paper
scissors
small, sharp knife
dressmaker's pin
paperclip
wire cutters
baking tray
paintbrushes
watercolour paints
matt varnish
coloured string or fine ribbon

1 Roll the dough out on baking parchment to a thickness of 1 cm (½ in). Scale up the template, transfer it to tracing paper and cut it out. Place on the dough and cut out the shape. Neaten the cut edges. Transfer the design details by pricking along the lines with a pin. Lightly moisten the pricked lines, then draw along them with the tip of the knife, leaning the blade to either side to mould the indentations.

2 Cut a paperclip in half with wire cutters and insert the two loops into the cut edges where marked, leaving the loops just visible. Transfer the angel, on the parchment, to a baking tray and bake at 120°C/250°F/Gas ½ for 10 hours. Allow to cool.

3 Paint the angel with water-colour paints, mixing the colours with white to lighten them and applying the paint thinly. Leave the flesh areas unpainted, but tint the cheek with a little pink. When the paint has dried, apply five coats of varnish. Hang the angel on coloured string or fine ribbon.

HARVEST WHEATSHEAF

*The golden sheaf of wheat makes an ideal decoration for
a kitchen wall, but remember to keep it away from steam.*

MATERIALS

tracing paper
pencil
card (cardboard) or paper for template
scissors
1 quantity salt dough
rolling pin
baking parchment
small, sharp knife
modelling tool (optional)
baking tray
paintbrush
satin varnish

TIP

To braid four strands of dough, lay
the first strand over the second,
and the third over the fourth. Then
lay what is now the third strand
back over the new second strand.
Repeat these two steps until the
braid is complete.

1 Scale up the template and cut it
out. Roll the dough out on
baking parchment to a thickness of
1 cm (½ in) and use the template to
cut out the wheatsheaf shape. Roll
out 12 cm (4¾ in) strands of dough
and build them up into a bundle.

2 Roll four 12 cm (4¾ in) strands
and join them at one end. Braid
the four strands. Moisten one side of
the braid and position it over the
bundle of stalks. Tuck the ends
neatly underneath.

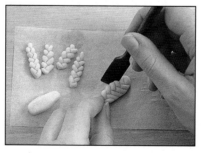

3 For ears of corn, roll sausages
from the dough, each measuring
3 x 1 cm (1¼ x ½ in). Flatten them
slightly and use a knife or modelling
tool to shape the grains. The sheaf
will need up to 50 ears.

4 Dampen the edge of the base
and build up rows of ears in
overlapping layers. Transfer, on
parchment, to a baking tray and
bake at 120°C/250°F/Gas ½ for 10
hours. Apply five coats of varnish.

ANGEL FRAME

Make this miniature frame, with its applied folk-art motifs, to enclose
a picture of your own little angel.

MATERIALS

1 quantity salt dough
rolling pin
baking parchment
pencil
tracing paper
card (cardboard) or paper for template
scissors
small, sharp knife
pair of compasses
drinking straw
scrap of corrugated cardboard
paintbrushes
watercolour paints
satin varnish

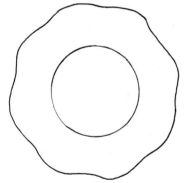

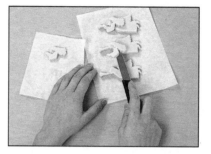

1 Roll out the dough, on baking parchment, to a thickness of 1 cm (½ in). Scale up the templates and cut out the frame, three angels and three hair and arm shapes from the dough. Place the hair and arm pieces on top of the angels and indent the details with the knife tip.

2 Roll the remaining dough to a thickness of 5 mm (¼ in). Cut a circle 10.5 cm (4⅛ in) in diameter to form the back of the frame. Cut a narrow strip 1 cm (½ in) wide. Lay it around half the circle. Pierce two holes in the circle for hanging, using the drinking straw.

3 Bake the frame and the angels at 120°C/250°F/Gas ½ for 1 hour. Moisten the underside of the angels and smear them with dough. Press the angels on to the frame. Bake the frame and the circle for 8 hours.

4 Smear the top of the semicircle with dough. Put corrugated cardboard at the top of the circle. Press the frame on to the backing circle. Bake for 2 hours. Remove cardboard. Paint and apply five coats of varnish.

STRAWBERRY CLOCK

Richly coloured tartan provides the perfect foil for glowing red strawberries,
which take the place of the numerals on this original clock.

MATERIALS

1 quantity salt dough
rolling pin
baking parchment
small, sharp knife
baking tray
drill and bit
paintbrushes
acrylic gesso or matt emulsion
(flat latex) paint
acrylic or craft paints
gloss varnish
clock movement and hands

1 Roll the dough out on baking parchment to a thickness of 2.5 cm (1 in). Cut out a rectangle with a sharp knife. Mould seven strawberry shapes (three large, four small), and prick seed markings with the knife. Moisten the strawberries and attach the large ones to the top of the rectangle and the smaller ones in place of the 3, 6, 9 and 12 on the clock face. Transfer the clock, on the parchment, to a baking tray and bake at 120°C/ 250°F/Gas ½ for 8 hours until hard.

2 Remove from the oven and allow to cool. Drill a hole in the centre. Apply a coat of acrylic gesso or matt emulsion (flat latex) paint and allow to dry before painting the clock face and the strawberries. Apply five coats of gloss varnish.

3 Decorate the hands of the clock with dots of paint. When dry, fit the movement and hands to complete the clock.

WINDOW ORNAMENTS

These stylish decorations catch the light beautifully when hung in a window.
The stained-glass effect is created from melted boiled sweets (hard candies).

MATERIALS

pencil
scissors
card (cardboard) or paper for template
1 quantity salt dough
rolling pin
baking parchment
small, sharp knife
flour for dusting
boiled sweets (hard candies)
cocktail stick (toothpick)
baking tray
paintbrushes
acrylic gesso or matt emulsion
(flat latex) paint
gold craft paint
satin varnish
fine gold cord

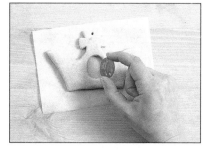

1 Draw and cut heraldic shapes out of thin card (cardboard). Roll the dough out on baking parchment to a thickness of 8 mm (⅜ in). Place the templates on the dough and cut out using a sharp knife. Lightly dust with flour and place a boiled sweet (hard candy) in the centre. Cut around it, adding a 2 mm (¹⁄₁₆ in) margin. Remove the sweet (hard candy) and lift out the piece of dough.

2 Pierce a hole in the top of each shape with a cocktail stick (toothpick). Transfer the models, on the parchment, to a baking tray and bake at 120°C/250°F/Gas ½ for 9 hours. Place a boiled sweet (hard candy) in each hole and return to the oven for 30 minutes, then let cool.

3 Undercoat the dough with acrylic gesso or matt emulsion (flat latex) paint and allow to dry. Paint the shapes with gold craft paint. Apply five coats of satin varnish. Hang the decorations from fine gold cord.

EASTER EGG BASKET

This little basket full of bright eggs makes a pretty seasonal decoration to hang on the wall.

MATERIALS

1 quantity salt dough
aluminium foil
rolling pin
small, sharp knife
fork
baking tray
paintbrushes
acrylic paints
gloss varnish
ribbon

2 Roll some sausages of dough and twist together to make the handle and basket trim. Moisten the surfaces and attach to the basket. Cut out a thin square of dough, cut in half diagonally and drape the triangles over the edge of the basket. Transfer the basket, on the foil, to a baking tray and bake at 120°C/250°F/Gas ½ for 8 hours until hard.

1 Mould four walnut-sized eggs and four half eggs from dough and arrange on a sheet of aluminium foil. Fold another sheet of foil into a basket shape. Roll out the remaining dough to a thickness of 5 mm (¼ in). Cut out a semicircle and mark a weave pattern on it with a fork. Arrange on the folded foil.

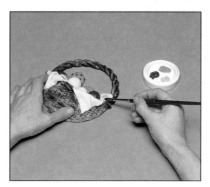

3 Using acrylic paints, colour the basket and handle in shades of brown and the eggs with a variety of bright patterns. When the basket is dry, apply five coats of gloss varnish. Tie a ribbon loop around the handle to hang up the basket.

CHRISTMAS WREATH MOBILE

Add this pretty mobile, hung with traditional Yuletide images, to your collection of Christmas ornaments. Use festive red and green ribbons to trim and hang the shapes.

MATERIALS

1 quantity salt dough
knitting needle
rolling pin
baking parchment
holly leaf pastry cutter
aluminium foil
baking tray
paintbrushes
acrylic paints
strong, clear glue
gloss varnish
1 m (3 ft 3 in) red ribbon,
6 mm (¼ in) wide
2.5 m (8 ft 4 in) green ribbon,
3 mm (⅛ in) wide
brass ring

TIP

You could use any small motif to make your own original mobile design: a medley of fruits for the kitchen or colourful characters for a child's room.

1 Use half of the dough to make the large wreath by twisting two rolls together. Make three small wreaths in the same way with one-third of the remaining dough. Make eight evenly spaced holes around the large wreath and a small hole in each of the small wreaths. With half of the remaining dough make three icicles by folding rolled lengths of dough in half and twisting. Leave a gap at the top for the ribbon.

2 Roll out the remaining dough on baking parchment and cut out four holly leaves. Roll tiny berries from the trimmings. Make a small hole in each leaf and shape over foil. Place all the shapes, on the parchment, on a baking tray and bake at 120°C/250°F/Gas ½ for 8 hours.

3 When cool, paint the icicles, holly leaves and berries with acrylic paint. Glue the holly leaves in pairs and add the berries to them. Allow to dry, then apply five coats of gloss varnish to all the pieces.

4 Tie a red ribbon bow to each small wreath. Cut the green ribbon into 30 cm (12 in) lengths and tie a knot 14 cm (5½ in) along each length. Thread the ribbons through the holes in the large wreath and tie the ends to the brass ring. Tie on the leaves, icicles and wreaths.

DINOSAUR

The ponderous character of this stegosaurus comes over clearly when modelled in chunky salt dough. When baked, the surface texture of the dough looks just right for dinosaur hide.

MATERIALS

wire cutters
tape measure
small-gauge chicken wire
pliers
pencil
card (cardboard) or paper for template
scissors
2 x quantity salt dough
rolling pin
tracing paper
baking parchment
small, sharp knife
baking tray
aluminium foil
masking tape
2 glass beads
paintbrushes
watercolour paints
matt varnish

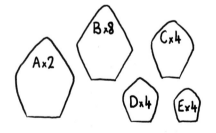

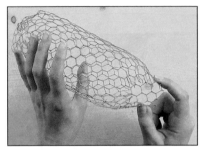

1 Use wire cutters to cut a 29 x 24 cm (11½ x 9½ in) rectangle from chicken wire for the body. Bend into a tube with the short sides meeting and hook together with pliers to hold the shape. Squeeze the ends of the tube to form an oval. Cut rectangles of 25 x 14 cm (10 x 5½ in) for the tail and 14 x 10 cm (5½ x 4 in) for the head. Bend into tubes with the short sides meeting.

2 Cut four 8 x 7 cm (3¼ x 2¾ in) rectangles for the legs. Make into tubes with the short sides meeting. Position under the body and hook into place. Hook on the tail and bend it around the body, tapering the end. Attach the head and squeeze the end to narrow it. Check that the model will fit into the oven, allowing for the plates and spines on top.

3 Scale up the plate templates and cut out. Roll out the dough on baking parchment to a thickness of 5 mm (¼ in). Cut out two size A plates, eight size B plates, and four each of sizes C, D and E. Round the cut edges and indent the veins.

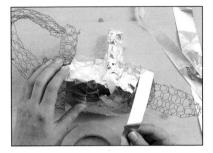

4 Roll four sausages of dough 4.5 cm (1¼ in) long for spines. Taper one end and bend into a curve. Transfer the plates and spines, on parchment, to a baking tray and bake at 120°C/250°F/Gas ½ for 3 hours. Meanwhile, bind strips of aluminium foil around the wire armature (frame) and secure with masking tape. Spread dough along the top of the dinosaur, building it up on the model's back.

5 Insert the plates in pairs, facing outwards, placing the largest in the centre. Tape the pairs together to hold them upright. Insert the spines in the same way on the tail. Bake for 2 hours, then add more dough to the model.

6 Embed beads for eyes and mark the mouth and nostrils with a knife. Bake for a further 2 hours. Continue smoothing on more dough and baking until the dinosaur is covered with dough and thoroughly hardened. Allow to cool completely, then paint with watercolour paints. Apply five coats of matt varnish.

CHECKER BOARD

Realistic lizards scamper around the edges of this unusual game board.
It's simple to make and will provide a talking point even when not in use.

MATERIALS

2 x quantity salt dough
rolling pin
baking parchment
small, sharp knife
ruler
pencil
paper
scissors
dressmaker's pins
baking tray
shells
paintbrushes
watercolour paints
satin varnish

1 Roll the dough out on baking parchment to a thickness of 1 cm (½ in). Using a knife and a ruler, cut a rectangle measuring 31 x 22.5 cm (12¼ x 8½ in) for the board. Round the cut edges. Cut a 20 cm (8 in) square of paper. Place it centrally on the dough and mark the corners and centre of each side with dressmaker's pins. Remove the paper.

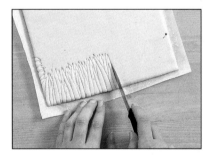

2 Moisten the edges of the rectangle and draw grass on the dough with the tip of a knife, allowing the grass to overlap the area of the square. Remove the pins as you work.

3 Roll two sausages of dough 8 x 2 cm (3¼ x ¾ in) for the lizards. Narrow one end of each to a point to form a tail. Draw a 22.5 x 6 cm (8½ x 2¼ in) rectangle on baking parchment and arrange the lizards within this shape, linking their tails. Shape the heads.

4 Roll four 1 cm (½ in) balls of dough for each lizard. Roll into sausages and bend in half. Fix to the lizards to make legs. Flatten the ends and cut into four toes. Indent the eyes with a pin head. Repeat to make two more lizards. Place on a baking tray.

5 Bake the board and the lizards at 120°C/250°F/Gas ½ for 1 hour. Allow to cool, then smear the undersides of the lizards with dough and fix to the board. Bake for a further 9 hours. Meanwhile, roll 24 balls 1 cm (½ in) in diameter for the counters. Flatten them and impress with shell patterns. Bake for 4 hours.

6 Paint the lizards, grass and counters with watercolours. Paint the board centre white and divide this area into eight rows of eight 2.5 cm (1 in) squares, allowing the outer squares to extend into the foliage. Paint alternate squares black. Allow to dry. Apply five coats of satin varnish.

FLOTILLA OF BOATS

Set sail with a colourful group of weather-beaten boats reminiscent of traditional nautical models. Metal studs or brass eyelets for portholes add a finishing touch.

MATERIALS

aluminium foil
masking tape
baking parchment
1 quantity salt dough
metal studs or eyelets (optional)
screw eyes (optional)
skewer
fine wood dowelling
baking tray
paintbrushes
acrylic gesso or matt emulsion
(flat latex) paint
acrylic or craft paints
burnt sienna Indian ink (optional)
fine-grade sandpaper
matt varnish
fabric scraps
PVA (white) glue
scissors
craft knife
thick thread (optional)
large-eyed sewing needle (optional)

1 Scrunch a piece of aluminium foil loosely into a ball. Mould it into a boat shape by pressing against a hard surface. Mould a smaller piece into a cube to make a cabin and fix on with masking tape. Working on baking parchment, press dough around the sides and top to a thickness of about 5 mm (¼ in). Gently press metal studs or eyelets into the sides of the boat if you wish. Insert screw eyes in the ends if you wish to hoist some pennants.

2 To add a mast, pierce a hole in the top of the boat with a skewer, then push in a length of dowelling. Press the dough around the base to hold it steady. Make a variety of boats and transfer, on baking parchment, to a baking tray. Bake at 120°C/250°F/Gas ½ for 4½ hours. Upturn the boats and cover the bases in dough, then bake for a further 4½ hours. Allow to cool.

3 Prime with acrylic gesso or matt emulsion (flat latex) paint, then decorate with acrylic or craft paints. Paint the masts with burnt sienna Indian ink if you wish. Gently sand the boats to add a sense of wear and tear. Apply five coats of varnish. Paint fabric scraps with PVA (white) glue and cut out flags and pennants. Glue a flag to the top of each mast.

4 Use a craft knife to cut a slit across the top of the masts to take a string of pennants, if adding. Tie a length of thick thread to one screw eye, and thread it through the pennants using a large-eyed needle. Slot into the mast and tie to the other screw eye.

THREE LITTLE PIGS

Small children will be captivated by this trio of salt-dough pigs to hang on the nursery wall. Have fun giving each of them different clothes and accessories.

MATERIALS

baking parchment
1 quantity salt dough
paperclips
small, sharp knife
skewer
rolling pin
small circular cutter
garlic press
baking tray
paintbrushes
acrylic or craft paints
satin varnish

1 Working on a sheet of baking parchment, make the first pig's head and body from balls of dough and press a paperclip into the head as a hanger. Roll sausage shapes and cut into lengths for the snout, arms and legs. Snip the ends of the arms and legs to make trotters and indent the "ankles" with a knife.

2 Make creases on the snout, moisten and stick in position. Use a skewer to mark the eyes and nostrils. Roll out the remainder of the dough thinly. Cut a circle with the circular cutter, make ears from semicircles, then stick the ears in position.

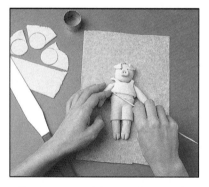

3 Cut out a wide vest shape and trousers and position over the front of the pig, turning the edges under to neaten them.

4 Squeeze some dough through a garlic press to make the bundle of sticks and add the remaining details such as buttons and belt. Make the other two pigs in the same way. Transfer, on the parchment, to a baking tray and bake at 120°C/250°F/Gas ½ for 8 hours. Allow to cool before decorating with acrylic or craft paints. To finish, apply five coats of satin varnish.

ANIMAL FINGER PUPPETS

Guaranteed to entertain and easy to make, these colourful and amusing finger puppets are constructed over card (cardboard) cones.

tracing paper
pencil
card (cardboard) or paper for templates
thin card (cardboard)
scissors
masking tape
pair of compasses
1 quantity salt dough
small, sharp knife
pastry wheel (optional)
2 wooden cocktail sticks (toothpicks)
6 small and 4 larger glass beads for eyes
rolling pin
toy-making whiskers
baking parchment
baking tray
paintbrushes
acrylic gesso or matt emulsion
(flat latex) paint
acrylic or craft paints
small natural sponge
satin varnish
stranded embroidery thread
scrap of brown long-haired fur fabric
strong, clear glue

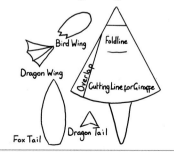

1 Scale up the templates and transfer to card (cardboard). You will need five basic puppet shapes, separate tails for the fox and dragon, two dragon's wings and two bird's wings. Bend the shapes into cones and secure with tape. Bend over each point at the fold line to form the head.

2 Cut quarter-circles of card (cardboard) with a radius of 6 cm (2¼ in). Bend into cones and tape. Support the puppets on these cones while you cover them with dough. Decorate the dragon's body with a knife or pastry wheel to score lines. Cut two slits for the wings.

3 Roll two small balls and press in place as nostrils, indenting with a cocktail stick (toothpick). Roll two 1 cm (½ in) balls and press in two larger beads for eyes. Indent the mouth. Cut out two wings and a tail from thin dough. Create the crocodile's face in the same way. For the giraffe, cut two short lengths from a cocktail stick (toothpick) and insert into the top of its head. Pierce a hole in the base for the tail. Press on ears, small beads for eyes, and a mouth.

4 To make the fox, cut 5 cm (2 in) lengths of whiskers, moisten the snout and place them on top. Roll a small ball of dough for a nose and press to the top of the snout, sandwiching the whiskers. Press on ears and small beads for eyes. Mould wing shapes for the seagull and press on two small beads for eyes.

5 Stand the pieces on parchment on a baking tray and bake at 120°C/250°F/Gas ½ for 3 hours. Fold the dragon's wings along the "veins" and insert the moistened ends into the slits on the body. Moisten the tail and press on. Bake for 5 hours. Paint with acrylic gesso or matt emulsion (flat latex) paint, then decorate using the natural sponge to apply acrylic or craft paints. Apply five coats of varnish.

6 To make the giraffe's tail, cut three lengths of stranded embroidery thread. Thread these through the hole and knot the ends inside the puppet. Braid the threads and knot the ends together; fray the ends. To make the fox's tail, use the tail template to cut out the fur fabric and glue to the salt dough tail.

MAKING SALT DOUGH

The basic recipe for salt dough is very easy to remember. If you wish, you can add 15 ml (1 tablespoon) of vegetable oil to the mixture to make it more supple, while 15 ml (1 tablespoon) of wallpaper paste will give extra elasticity. You will find it easier to make large quantities of dough in several batches. Keep made-up dough in an airtight container to prevent it drying out. It will keep in the fridge for up to a week, but let it return to room temperature before you begin to work with it.

INGREDIENTS

2 cups plain (all-purpose) flour
1 cup salt
1 cup water

1 Mix together the flour, salt and half the water in a mixing bowl. Knead the mixture, gradually adding more water until the dough has a smooth, firm consistency. Be careful not to add too much water or the dough will sag and become sticky.

2 Remove the dough from the bowl and continue to knead for 10 minutes. The dough can be modelled immediately, but is best left to "rest" for 30 minutes in an airtight container. Bake the salt dough in a domestic oven at 120°C/250°F/ Gas ½, until the model is completely hardened all over. Allow it to cool slowly before working on it further.

TINTING AND MARBLING SALT DOUGH

Salt dough takes various kinds of paint very well, or you may find its natural colour pleasing for some projects. In some cases, you may wish to colour the dough before modelling it.

1 Make a central well in the dough and add some food colouring. Fold the dough over and knead it thoroughly until it is evenly coloured, adding more colouring if necessary to achieve the desired shade. To colour a large amount of dough, break it into small pieces and colour each one separately, kneading it together finally to achieve a uniform tone.

2 To marble the colours, roll differently coloured pieces of dough into sausages of equal size. Twist the sausages together and then knead to blend the colours. Be careful not to overdo the kneading or the veining effect will be lost. Try creating new colours by blending two shades together.

ROLLING OUT THE DOUGH

Roll salt dough out flat with a rolling pin on a lightly floured surface such as a chopping board, or on a sheet of baking parchment. If the dough sticks to the rolling pin, sprinkle on a little flour.

SCALING-UP

Draw your own templates for the projects in this book, or scale up those provided to the required size. If you have access to a photocopier it will do the job for you. Otherwise, copy the template on to tracing paper, draw a squared grid over it, and transfer the template, square by square, on to a sheet of larger scale graph paper.

INDEX

Publisher's Acknowledgements:
The publishers would like to thank the
following people:

Contributors: Petra Boase, Jan Bridge
Lucinda Ganderton, Ariane Gastambide,
Anna Griffiths, Rachel Howard, Julie
Johnson, Cheryl Owen, Carol Pastor, Bee
Smithwick, Catherine Whitfield, Emma
Whitfield, Josephine Whitfield, Isabella
Whitworth, Dorothy Wood

Photographers: Madeleine Brehaut, James
Duncan, Mark Gatehouse, Lucy Mason,
Martin Norris, Debbie Patterson, Steve
Tanner, Lucy Tizard, Shona Wood